Baby Shower Planning Like A Pro

A Step-by-Step Guide on How to Plan & Host the Perfect Baby Shower. Baby Shower Themes, Games, Gifts Ideas, & Checklist Included

Katherine Smiley
Copyright© 2014 by Katherine Smiley

Baby Shower Planning Like A Pro

Publisher: Enlightened Publishing

ISBN-13: 978-1499271089

ISBN-10: 1499271085

60943057

Disclaimer

The Publisher has strived to be as accurate and complete as possible in the creation of this book. While all attempts have been made to verify information provided in this publication, the Publisher assumes no responsibility for errors, omissions, or contrary interpretation of the subject matter herein. Any perceived slights of specific persons, peoples, or organizations are unintentional.

This book is not intended for use as a source of legal, business, accounting or financial advice. All readers are advised to seek services of competent professionals in the legal, business, accounting, and finance fields.

Table of Contents

Introduction

If your family member, good friend or co-worker is expecting a baby soon, you're of course feeling very excited and happy for them. As you eagerly help them pick out everything from baby names to paint colors for their new nursery, there is one important event to consider that requires advance planning and some creativity. This event is of course the baby shower.

Traditionally, a baby shower is thrown by a close friend or female family member who is not the mother of the mom-to-be. These days baby showers are frequently thrown by more than one hostess, which helps to lessen the financial burden and time spent for any one individual hostess. Some moms-to-be find themselves being honored by more than one baby shower. For example, a soon-to-be mom may be given a baby shower at her place of employment by her co-workers, as well as a more personal baby shower at the home of a close friend or family member.

If you're reading this baby shower guide, you are most likely planning to host a baby shower for someone and looking for some guidance. Whether you volunteered to throw a baby shower or someone asked you to do so, throwing a baby shower can be a fun but rather daunting task. The birth of a baby is one of the most momentous occasions that can happen in life, so you want the baby shower to be fun, creative and completely worthy of the exciting new life event. This may sound like a lot of pressure, but don't worry. It's absolutely possible to throw an amazing baby shower without becoming overwhelmed or going broke.

Baby showers are joyous occasions, but also involve a lot of planning and work. If you're looking for a fun, easy to follow, step-by-step guide to planning and hosting a baby shower, look no further--you're definitely in the right place. By the end of this guide you'll be well on your way to hosting a fun, special, and best of all low-stress baby shower for your friend or loved one.

This guide includes everything from theme ideas, decorations, games and activities to menu planning advice and baby shower etiquette. There's even a handy checklist at the end to make sure you stay on track and organized while planning the baby shower.

Whether you are planning a low-key, casual baby shower or a dressier, more formal brunch or dinner, there are tips here that will help you all along the way. The mom-to-be and her friends and family will be thrilled with your thoughtfulness, and you will feel the pride of being an integral part in celebrating this special time in her life.

History of Baby Showers

Baby showers are a sweet tradition with a long history. New babies have always been welcomed by society and families as exciting blessings, and so it makes sense that the tradition of throwing a baby shower for expectant mothers is an old one. Baby showers are not a tradition that is unique to the United States either, with families and communities the world over gathering to celebrate a new life and shower soon-to-be mothers with gifts and affection.

There is some evidence that baby showers were celebrated even as far back as the days of ancient Rome and Egypt. In those days, the women of the community or village would gather together to celebrate the new baby and would shower the new mother with hand-made gifts she could use once the baby arrived. These gifts commonly include baby blankets and clothes, which are still popular baby gifts today. While baby shower etiquette and activities have changed over time, getting together to celebrate a new life and "showering" the baby with gifts is a time-honored tradition indeed.

Baby showers as we know them today, complete with games and cake, became popular in the years just after World War II. This makes sense if you think about it, since the years just after World War II are now referred to as the "Baby Boom," or a time when record numbers of young people became married and started new families, looking to create stable, happy home lives after the tumultuous years of war. Nowadays baby showers are considered a great time to get together, enjoy some delicious food and drink, laugh and mingle, play silly games, and gather around in excitement as the mom-to-be opens gifts for herself and the new baby.

Chapter 1: Time to Get Planning

The early planning stage of hosting a baby shower is very important. If you get organized from the beginning of the planning stage your baby shower planning will be a piece of cake. Here's everything you need to know about planning the theme, deciding on the guest list, and more:

1. Who Hosts the Baby Shower?

Traditionally, the hostess of the baby shower had to be someone who was not related to the mom-to-be. The reasoning behind this old-fashioned etiquette rule was that if a relative of the mom-to-be threw the shower they would be seen as asking for gifts for the family, which was considered bad manners.

These days, that rule is often seen as dated and unnecessary, with many baby showers being thrown by female relatives of the mother-to-be, although it is still considered poor etiquette for the mother of the honored guest to host the baby shower. Often the hostess of the baby shower is a sister, best friend or female cousin. Ideally, the hostess of the shower offers to throw it, although sometimes the hostess is asked to do so by the mom-to-be.

It is also becoming more common for multiple people to host the shower together. For example, the mom-to-be's best friend and sisters might get together to plan the shower. This can be a great idea since it means the cost of the shower as well as the planning can be divided among more than one person, making hosting a baby shower easier and more affordable.

2. Decide on the type of baby shower. Casual or more formal? Co-ed or ladies only?

Before you start considering specific themes or decorations, you'll want to decide in a more general sense what type of baby shower you plan to throw. This decision should be made with the mom-to-be's wishes, taste, personality, and preferences in mind.

Here are a few variables to consider and decide on:

- **Casual or formal or somewhere in between?**

- **Time of day**: brunch, afternoon tea, dinner, cocktails and hors d'oeuvres? Typically, the earlier in the day the less formal the occasion, although this isn't always the case.

- **Co-ed or all women?** While baby showers have traditionally been women only affairs, in recent years co-ed baby showers have become more common. Co-ed baby showers tend to be more relaxed and informal. Co-ed baby showers also tend to include less of the traditional baby shower games and activities, as these don't always appeal to men. Many women prefer the more traditionally feminine atmosphere of a women-only baby shower. A compromise that allows for a women-only shower but still lets the men feel included is to hold a traditional female-only shower, but invite the dad-to-be and any close male family members or friends to join the celebration at the end. At this time the party can shift from a more traditional baby shower to a more laid-back party atmosphere, with beer and guy-friendly snacks.

- **First baby or not?** Generally speaking, a baby shower for first time parents tends to be larger and more involved than a baby shower for parents who already have children. Baby showers for parents who already have children tend to be simpler and less elaborate. The reasoning behind this is that if the parents already have children, they will likely already have a lot of the necessary baby items, such as a crib, a stroller, clothes, etc. Exceptions to this general rule include situations where there is a large age difference between the older children and the baby (since this lessens the chances that the parents still have lots of baby stuff on hand) or sometimes if the new baby is a different gender from the other children.

- **Surprise?** While most baby showers are held with the mom-to-be's knowledge and input, surprise baby showers are increasingly common. Only throw a surprise baby shower if you know that the mother-to-be takes surprises well, as some people definitely do not.

To pull off a surprise baby shower you will need to enlist the help of her husband and possibly one or more of her close friends or family members. Someone will need to invent an event to invite her to during the day and time of the shower, to make sure she will not make other plans during that time. Ideally, the pretend event will require her to dress up a little bit and look her best, so that she won't be embarrassed by her appearance when she realizes you've thrown a surprise shower for her.

You will also need to know her well enough to have a good handle on her general taste and preferences, in order to throw a baby shower that she would love without asking for her input. While hosting a surprise baby shower does present some challenges, it can also be incredibly fun, and the look of shocked delight on the mother-to-be's face when she walks into her surprise shower will make all the challenges worth it.

The best way to determine the style and tone of the baby shower is to ask the mom-to-be. After all, she is the reason you are throwing the shower. Be sure not to impose your own vision for the day onto her against her will. You will have plenty of time to express your own creativity when planning the decorations, activities, and menu, after all.

3. Guest List: Who to Invite?

This is another aspect of the baby shower that should be left up to the soon to be mother, perhaps with input from her immediate family. If she would like to invite all of her female family members including distant cousins and great aunts, co-workers, and miscellaneous acquaintances, that is her prerogative.

On the other hand, if she would prefer to keep the baby shower smaller and more intimate, that is also her right. In many cases the mother of the mom-to-be also has input into the guest list, perhaps wishing to invite a few of her close friends who have watched the mom-to-be grow up since she was a little girl. This can be a great way to honor the mother-daughter bond as well as create a true family feel for the event.

While it should be up to the mother-to-be to plan the guest list, as the hostess of the shower you shouldn't feel pressured to make or purchase food for a hundred people if that's beyond the scope of your budget or available time. Openly and respectfully communicate any concerns that you have about budget or logistics relating to the guest list, and come to a solution with the mother-to-be. In some cases the mother-to-be or her family may offer to help shoulder the costs of the baby shower, especially if they insist on inviting a great many people and therefore increasing the cost of the baby shower.

This is also the time when the earlier decision to make the baby shower women-only or co-ed comes into play, since this decision will affect the guest list. If having a co-ed baby shower, any couples on the guest list should just receive a single invitation addressed to them both of course.

If you are planning a surprise baby shower, you will need the help of her significant other and probably her family in order to gather the names and addresses of everyone you should invite.

4. Where Will You Throw the Baby Shower?

Traditionally, baby showers have been thrown in the home of the hostess, which provides guests with a comfortable, homey and intimate environment. While this is still a great option for a baby shower location, these days many baby shower hostesses are thinking outside of the box and scouting out new and different locations.

Some possible locations for a baby shower include restaurants (especially if you can reserve a private room), parks, churches, community centers, and even bars, especially for co-ed baby showers. Some with larger budgets have even thrown baby showers as overnight events at a nice hotel with spa services.

The location can really be nearly anywhere, but should be determined based on the feeling or tone you are looking to create as well as your budget. For example, a dressy tea party shower probably shouldn't take place at a sport's bar or noisy park, but would be perfect at the hostess' home or in a nice restaurant.

Generally, hosting the baby shower in your home or someone else's home will be the most cost-effective approach.

5. Setting the Date

Another important aspect of the early stages of baby shower planning is finding the perfect date for the big event. Baby showers are typically thrown towards the end of pregnancy, three or four weeks before the baby's due date. Throwing the baby shower too early in the pregnancy before the mom-to-be has a dramatically pregnant belly to show off can seem less exciting. It can also place too much pressure on the mom-to-be to make decisions about decorating her nursery, etc., since she will likely want to include some nursery items on her baby shower gift registry.

The end of pregnancy is an exciting time and also when the mom-to-be has the clearest idea of what baby things she still needs, so this is probably the best time to throw the shower. Always leave at least a couple of weeks between the shower and the due date, however, in case the baby decides to show up a little early.

Other things to consider when setting the date are commonly celebrated holidays (it's best to avoid throwing a shower right around Christmas or Easter, for example, when many guests will have other plans or be traveling) or any other big life events that the family of the mother-to-be already has planned. You should probably ask about any upcoming weddings or graduations in the family, for example, in order to plan around them.

Another thing to consider is throwing a baby shower after the baby is born. This is a definite break from tradition, but is something that is starting to be considered more and more by some parents-to-be. One of the potential benefits to hosting a shower after the baby is born is that the guests will all get to meet the new baby. Another possible benefit is that some parents prefer to wait until after the baby is born to learn its sex. Knowing the baby's sex can make it easier to plan the baby shower decor as well as pick out gifts for the baby, since these things are often gender-specific.

6. Invitations

There are a ton of different options these days for baby shower invitations. You can buy premade, fill-in-the-blank invites where you just fill in the information for your baby shower and drop them in the mail.

On the other end of the spectrum are custom invitations that you can order from specialty shops online or brick and mortar stationery stores. These will cost more money but add a highly stylish, personalized touch, especially for more formal baby shower occasions.

Some baby shower hostesses get extra creative and send physical objects as invites- think miniature baby bottle with the baby shower details tucked away inside the bottle.

Sending an electronic invitation by email is the most affordable and easy option and nowadays is increasingly considered a perfectly acceptable option from an etiquette standpoint. Email invitations come in a wide range of color schemes and designs and also allow for a simplified RSVP process. If the mom-to-be's elderly relatives are invited, however, you may still need to send them a paper invitation or at least invite by them phone, since many elderly people do not use email.

Here are a few things to keep in mind when picking out, customizing, and sending your baby shower invitations:

- Be sure to send out invitations at least 2 or 3 weeks before the shower, to help ensure that most guests don't already have plans and allow them time to shop for the perfect baby gift.

- Consider including a cute baby-related poem or saying in the invitations. You can find many examples online if you're stuck. Here is one to get you started:

    "Is it a girl or is it a boy?
    When they arrive they'll bring such joy!
    Ten little fingers, ten little toes
    So sweet and cuddly, right down to their nose"

- Don't forget to include any of the basic info: mom-to-be's name, date and time of shower, location and address of baby shower, RSVP info, and registry information (optional).

- If any of the games or activities planned for the shower requires guests to bring something or be prepared ahead of time, it's a good idea to include this information in the invitation. For example, if you play the game where guests try to identify baby pictures of other guests (see our Games and Activities section for details) you will want to mention this in the invitation so that your guests know to bring a picture of themselves as a baby.

- If there are any specific instructions relating to gifts, be sure to include them in the invitation. For example, sometimes the parents-to-be wish to encourage their guests to bring a specific item, such as diapers, children's books, or baby bath time items. This can be part of a special theme for the baby shower, or just a general recommendation or request.

- When budgeting for invitations make sure to include the cost of stamps. If you're inviting a lot of people or have heavy or non-standard sized invitations you will quickly go through a lot of stamps and may be surprised by how expensive they can be. You can order customized baby shower stamps online for a personalized touch.

- If you are hand addressing the invitations and inviting a lot of people, consider asking a friend or two for help. You can have a small get-together and make this tedious task go by much more quickly. Just make sure that the friends you ask for help have nice, neat, legible handwriting of course.

- Remember to include a name, phone number and/or email address for people to respond to the invitation with their RSVP. Stay organized and keep a running list of how many people are coming. If you send electronic invitations this part will be much simpler, as most electronic invite sites, like Evite.com for example, track your RSVPs for you.

- Including gift registry information on invitations used to be considered bad manners, but these days most people consider it acceptable (and helpful) information to include on the invitation or as an additional small insert inside the envelope. As long as the expectant parents are registered somewhere and are okay with you sharing this information, go ahead and include it in the invitations. This will make gift shopping easier for guests and help to eliminate too many duplicate or unwanted presents.

- If there's a theme (see upcoming chapter) you might want to mention it on the invitations. This gives guests the chance to coordinate their gift or the gift's wrapping paper and card with the theme if they wish to do so. Likewise, you might consider mentioning any nursery decorating theme the parents-to-be have chosen. For example, if they are decorating the nursery with a "nursery rhyme" or "baby bird" theme guests might like the chance to include a small decorative gift that fits this motif.

7. Deciding on a Theme

Having a theme for the baby shower is not mandatory, but it can be a great way to give everything a cute, cohesive look. It can also make planning much easier because you can use the theme as a guide for picking out everything from the invitations to decorations to the games. Plates, napkins, balloons, invitations and party favors that coordinate with your theme will make the event seem especially well put-together.

A sweet, thoughtful way to choose a theme is to ask the expectant mother if she has a theme in mind for the nursery. If she does, it's a good idea to have the baby shower in the same theme because then she can have the option of re-using many of the decorative items from the baby shower for the nursery.

If you'd rather not have a theme for the baby shower, you should at least decide on a color scheme of two or three complementary colors and do your best to stick to this scheme when picking out invitations and decorations. This will help give everything a cohesive look and prevent clashing colors.

If you'd like to give your baby shower a specific theme but aren't sure where to start, here are several fun ideas to inspire you:

- **Baby Animals** is one of the cutest baby shower themes out there. Decorations, paper plates, napkins and invitations with cute pictures of baby animals are easy to find online or at party planning stores. You can use a variety of baby animals or pick a single one, like bunnies or lambs. This theme can even extend to animal cracker party favors and serving pigs-in-a-blanket as one of the appetizers.

- **A book-themed baby shower** is a cute idea, especially if the mom-to-be is a librarian or a teacher. Each guest can bring a children's book or two, either as the main gift or as an add-on to another gift. This is a great way to give a baby their own library of books. The books can be a combination of educational and fun.

Stacks of brightly colored children's books can be used as décor. Library card invitations are a unique and quirky idea. Customized bookmarks make great party favors. Guests can even read short passages from their favorite nursery rhymes or children's books. Book-themed baby showers are especially popular with parents-to-be who already have at least one child, as they may already have many of the basic necessities.

- **A cartoon theme**, like Winnie the Pooh is fun and accessible. Decorations with specific cartoon characters are readily available. Winnie the Pooh invitations and decorations can have a sweetly vintage look to them. A cake in the shape of Winnie the Pooh or another cartoon character is a special touch. This is an especially good idea if the mom-to-be happens to have a favorite cartoon.

- **A diaper-themed shower** is an increasingly popular idea. Everyone knows that new parents go through diapers at an extremely rapid rate, and that diapers can therefore be one of the biggest baby-related expenses. Throwing a baby shower where all of the guests bring diapers is a great way to help the new parents out, and can also come with cute decoration ideas.

The baby shower invitation can include cute pictures of diaper pins or even an actual diaper pin closing the invitation. Cloth diapers with cute decorative diaper pins can be hung on a clothesline as decoration. Just like book-themed baby showers, this theme is especially popular with parents who already have other children. They may already have things like a crib, stroller, and car seat, but every parent of a baby needs plenty of diapers.

- **The ABC's** make a cute and simple to put together theme. Pastel-colored alphabet letters can be incorporated into the invitations or strung up as a decorative banner. Colorful alphabet blocks make cute decorative objects for the tables. You can even make or purchase a mobile made from ABCs to hang over the table as a centerpiece. This is a very sweet touch as the mobile can then be re-used by the mom-to-be over the crib in the baby's nursery.

- **Birds or owls** have become a trendy baby shower theme. Decorating with baby birds or owls is something that can be easily carried through the invitations to the decor. Since baby bird and owl décor has become very popular for nurseries, the baby shower decorations can easily get a second use after the baby is born. Brightly painted bird cages make for cool decorations and can also be used to hold cards and well wishes for the soon-to-be mom.

- **A spa-themed baby shower** is a great way to treat the expectant mother to a touch of luxurious indulgence and relaxation before her baby comes. Whether the shower takes place at an actual spa or at home, both mom and baby can receive relaxing spa-themed gifts like soothing lavender vanilla lotions, CDs of relaxing world music or lullabies (which can soothe both mom and baby's nerves in the coming months), and soft, organic cotton robes, baby blankets and towels. If you are working with a larger budget, gift certificates for the expectant mom to have a pre-natal massage or pedicure make an extra special touch.

- **Tea party baby showers** are sweetly old-fashioned yet sophisticated. Who doesn't like to put on a pretty dress and sip an assortment of teas while dining on scones, clotted cream, lemon curd and finger sandwiches? Since tea and the traditional accompaniments are small and dainty, the guests will have no problem enjoying them while oohing and ah-ing over the expectant mom's gifts. Tins of herbal tea will make great party favors.

- **A Jungle Book** or safari-inspired baby shower has a lot of potential and can easily lead to a colorful, humorous and fun baby shower. Plates, decorations, wrapping paper and invitations can feature cute cartoon versions of wild jungle animals, like lions, tigers, monkeys, giraffes, elephants, zebras and hippos. You can even decorate your baby shower space with hanging vines (real ones or made from linked together construction paper rings) to really set the mood. Guests can bring stuffed, plush baby elephants, monkeys or giraffes as sweet jungle-themed gifts for the new baby.

- **A Fiesta-themed shower** is colorful and exciting. You can play spicy Latin music in the background and decorate with brightly colored plates and napkins. Miniature maracas, sombreros or cacti make great party favors. Consider serving traditional Mexican tres leches cake as one of the desserts. For lunch or dinner you could serve a taco or fajita bar, which is sure to be a crowd pleaser.

- **The Showered with Love** theme is a creative and unique idea. For this baby shower you will focus on all things rain shower for your decorations. Think brightly colored, decorative umbrellas or parasols, miniature rain boots and rain coats. The umbrella theme can be integrated into your invitations, plates, wrapping paper, and more.

- **The "She's About to Pop" theme** is funny, unexpected and comes with lots of decorating potential. This creative theme revolves around the saying "she's about to pop," which refers to a pregnant woman who's rapidly approaching birth. The invitations can include the words "she's about to pop," and include cute cartoon pictures of balloons, for a fun play on words.

To incorporate this funny theme into your entire baby shower, feature decorations and food that involve "pop" or "popping." Some ideas include lots of balloons (of course), cake pops as party favors, lollipops as party favors or decorations, and even popcorn. If really want to go all out with this theme you can even rent an old-fashioned popcorn machine like at a movie theater. This is a very versatile theme and balloons in particular are easy to include on the invitations, plates, banners and other decorative items.

- **A Twinkle Twinkle Little Star themed shower** is unique and sweet. You can include some of the words to Twinkle, Twinkle Little Star on your baby shower invitations, along with star imagery. Garlands made of sparkling stars make for magical decorations. Star cupcake toppers and star-decked plates will help tie the theme together.

- **A circus-themed baby shower** is festive and colorful. Think red and black striped fabric backdrops (like that of a circus tent), vintage-inspired invitations featuring circus animals or tents, plus decorations involving tigers, elephants, trapeze artists and bears. You can even serve fun, circus-inspired snacks or box them up as party favors. Some options include cotton candy (available in a range of colors to match your color scheme) and cute red and white boxes of popcorn for the guests to take home with them.

- **Flower-power** is a bright, cheerful, and easy to pull together baby shower theme. For this theme idea you will want to start with a colorful floral motif on the baby shower invitations. As far as decorations go, start with the obvious and make bunches of bright, beautiful flowers the focal point.

You can go with dramatic bouquets as centerpieces or simple, delicate flowers in scattered bud vases around the tables and in other places as well. Colorful balloons in flower-shapes are a great touch. You can even carry the flower design onto the plates, napkins, banners, and more if you want to.

Flower-shaped sugar cookies would make cute desserts or even party favors for your guests to take home. Another party favor idea is to give them packets of wildflower seeds with cute, customized labels as they are leaving. You can give the actual flowers to your guests as well, saving the best bouquet for the beaming mom-to-be.

- **Beach Baby** is a fun baby shower theme, especially for moms-to-be who live for beach time. There are lots of possibilities for this theme, including giving out little plastic pails and shovels (like what kids play with on the beach when making sand castles) filled with candy, flip-flops, sunglasses, or other goodies as party favors. You can find the pails and other items at a dollar store or discount party store for not a lot of money.

You can decorate with beautiful sea-shells and stick to an ocean-inspired color palette of turquoise and white. Your baby shower invitations can feature a beach scene or cartoon seashells. For centerpieces, try filling large hard plastic or glass vases with sand, topped with sea shells, or ocean-themed bath toys. Cute sailboats can also be easily incorporated into the décor.

Chapter 2: The Preparation Stage

1. Getting the Decorations Ready

When it comes to decorating for the baby shower, the sky is the limit. Decorating can be one of the most fun and creative aspects of throwing a shower. Depending on your taste, how much time you have, the theme of the baby shower, and the preferences of the expectant mom, you can keep the decorations simple and easy, or they can be completely elaborate. Decorations can be store-bought from online or a party supply store, handmade, or a combination of the two.

If the baby shower decorations you have in mind are elaborate or time-consuming to put together, it's best to start as early as possible. Another time-saving idea is to enlist the help of a few close girlfriends. You can invite them over for snacks and drinks, put on some fun, up-tempo music, and have a decoration making party in your living room. If you do this you can set up stations where each person handles one small aspect of putting together the decorations, and they quickly get assembled factory-style.

If you want to keep things simple and stress-free, store-bought decorations might be your best bet. You can simply search online or go to your local party supply store armed with your baby shower theme or color scheme. Look for things that go with the theme or colors you've picked out and simply start filling your (real or virtual) shopping cart with matching streamers, balloons, napkins, tablecloths, banners, etc.

If you're planning to make the decorations yourself, you have a lot of options. Crafting magazines and websites as well as sites like Pinterest are filled with décor inspiration. Depending on your comfort level with DIY projects, available time and budget you might be able to make everything from the invitations, to decorative banners and more. Remember as you are making or purchasing your baby shower decorations in the weeks leading up to the shower to keep everything organized. Set up what you can ahead of time and then carefully stash the decorations somewhere safe and easily accessible, like large plastic storage tubs or an unused linen closet. Having the decorations ready to go and set aside will make the day of the baby shower much less stressful.

Whether you decide to make your own decorations or buy them from the store, here are a handful of fresh decoration ideas:

- **Flowers**: One DIY decorative touch that anyone can handle putting together is fresh flowers. Simply buy inexpensive, colorful blooms at your local grocery store and arrange in vases or even Mason jars. The flowers will add pops of color and a touch of freshness to your baby shower décor, while taking virtually no time to put together. They can double as party favors- who wouldn't love to take home a sweet bouquet of fresh flowers for their kitchen table?

- **Balloons**: These are another great option for quick, easy decorations. You can get them to match any color scheme and they are very affordable. Rather than simply having them floating around (too much like a kid's birthday party), try tying them into elegant bunches, floating over the center of the buffet table as a sweet centerpiece. You can anchor them to the table by tying their strings to an alphabet block, children's book, or miscellaneous wrapped gift. This is a great way to tie the balloons into your overall theme. You can also try tying one to each chair. This looks especially elegant when the colors are one or two muted pastels.

- **Banners**: Banners are easy and make any space automatically festive. You can buy pre-made banners that say "It's a Boy!" or "It's a Girl" at many stores. Another option is to purchase or make a banner made from bunting, or brightly colored or calico flags made from cloth. These vintage-inspired banners have recently made a come-back and would make a darling addition to the baby's nursery once the shower ends.

- **Candles**: If your baby shower is in the late afternoon or evening, candles are a great, inexpensive way to add ambience. Tea lights in bright white or colorful holders can be sprinkled throughout the room to add a touch of elegant style. Another option is small votives inside of decorative lanterns placed on the table.

- **Streamers**: Streamers are very affordable and can add a great touch of color to the baby shower. Stick with one or two colors that coordinate with your theme or color scheme for a classy, up-to-date look.

- **Chairs**: While not strictly decorative, don't forget about the chairs. Whether you are having the shower at home or elsewhere you will want to make sure you have enough seating for everyone. If you're hosting the shower at your home and don't have enough chairs you should look into either renting them from a party supply company, or borrowing extra chairs from friends if you don't mind the mismatched look.

If you're hosting the shower at a park you will most likely only have picnic tables available for your use, but many parks have chairs available for rent and will even set them up for you for an additional fee. Chairs won't be a problem at a restaurant or bar, but you will of course want to communicate ahead of time with the restaurant to let them know how many chairs you need, as well as any seating arrangement preferences.

- **Centerpieces**: Your table won't look complete without a centerpiece that complements your baby shower theme and color scheme. Depending on your theme you can keep the centerpieces simple, such as assorted tall and short candles with holders in your baby shower colors, or simple floral bouquets. If you're having a tea party-themed baby shower, brightly colored, vintage-style tea tins, either alone or holding pretty flowers, make darling, simple to set up centerpieces.

A centerpiece that can easily double as a gift for the new baby's nursery is a mobile hanging just over the center of the table. If you're serving cupcakes at the baby shower, they can easily be turned into a festive (and delicious!) centerpiece. Simply arrange the cupcakes on a pretty cake stand in the center of the table. As long as the cupcakes are decorated in colors that work with your color scheme this is a lovely option.

Another adorable idea that also happens to be quite affordable is to put together a baby duck centerpiece. For this centerpiece idea, you simply buy a clear glass goldfish bowl or other clear vessel, line the bottom with marbles or glass stones in your baby shower colors, and then float little toy rubber duckies in the water.

2. Decide on the Menu

While great decorations will set the tone and add a festive air to your event, good food and drinks are guaranteed to make your guests happy and will be one aspect of your party they will all remember for a long time to come. The baby shower menu may be decided by the theme to some degree. For example, if you are throwing a tea party themed baby shower, you will most likely want to serve a variety of herbal teas and all the usual accoutrements, such as scones and tea sandwiches.

The time of day when you are throwing the shower also comes into play when planning the menu. If the shower is timed around lunch or dinner time, you will probably want to offer a more substantial selection of food. On the other hand, if your shower isn't being thrown near typical meal times you can probably get away with just offering desserts or small snacks with beverages.

The location of the baby shower is also important when planning the menu. If you are throwing the baby shower at a restaurant or bar you will want to coordinate ahead of time with the manager. They will most likely be able to customize a special menu for you if you wish.

If you're hosting the shower at a park or in a church hall, you may want to consider having it as a pot-luck where each guest brings one or two items, so that no one person gets stuck with the bulk of food preparation. In this case make sure to coordinate with everyone, perhaps by emailing around a sign-up sheet. This will help prevent having a baby shower where three people bring lasagna but no one brings drinks or dessert.

Since most baby showers are thrown in the home of the hostess though, here are some popular baby shower menu ideas that you can easily make or purchase:

Cake and punch

For a sweet and simple baby shower, sometimes only cake and punch are served. If this is your plan you may want to add a note that says "Cake and punch reception" to your invitations, so that guests don't show up hungry, expecting a more substantial spread.

Cake and punch are very popular at showers, so even if you are serving a lot of other food it's a good idea to consider including cake and punch on the menu since many guests may expect it. Plus, pretty much everyone loves cake, and cakes can be easily decorated in a way that complements your theme or color scheme. You can either make the cake yourself or order one from a bakery. There are tons of simple punch recipes available online. You will need to purchase or borrow a large punch bowl if you don't already own one.

Finger foods and appetizers

These are a great idea because you can offer your guests a large variety of things to snack on without going too overboard on preparations or busting your budget. Another benefit of an appetizers only baby shower is that your guests can eat while also easily walking around, mingling, and then watching the mom-to-be open her gifts. Some popular and delicious finger foods include pigs-in-a-blanket, bruschetta, good cheese and olives on skewers, deviled eggs, fruit skewers, chicken wings, shrimp skewers, and jalapeno poppers.

Buffet-style

If you plan to serve a full brunch, lunch or dinner at your baby shower, serving the food buffet-style is the way to go. It allows your guests to sit wherever they want, only get the food they want and mingle at will.

For a brunch buffet options include baked French toast, maple-glazed bacon, eggs benedict, scrambled eggs with goat cheese and mushrooms, quiche, and fruit salad. For lunch or dinner some familiar, buffet-friendly favorites include lasagna, baked mac and cheese, a big garden salad, warm French bread, fresh fruit and veggie trays, or you could even make a gourmet sandwich bar with all the deli fixings.

For a less traditional spread that will be sure to delight your guests, try serving a taco bar. Let your guests load up corn or flour tortillas, or hard taco shells, with taco meat, chicken, or fish, plus beans, rice and all the fixings. Make sure to offer a selection of salsas from mild to hot to please everyone's palate. A taco bar is a great idea for a fiesta-themed baby shower.

Dessert

For a late afternoon baby shower that falls in between lunch and dinner a dessert-only baby shower is a really fun idea that your guests will love. You can have trays arranged with an assortment of full-sized or miniature desserts, including cake, cheesecake, pastries, chocolate truffles, mini apple tarts, etc.

Another fun idea is to offer your guests an ice cream sundae bar. Everyone will love pretending they're kids again, piling chocolate, caramel or strawberry sauce over their bowl of ice cream. Small dishes of sprinkles, peanuts, sliced strawberries and bananas, and a large dish of homemade whipped cream are extra special touches.

Drinks

Don't forget the beverages! In addition to punch, you will probably want to have a variety of drinks on hand to suit different tastes. Champagne is often served at baby showers and makes the shower more festive. Even though the mother-to-be can't partake, her friends and family will love the chance to toast to her.

If you're serving brunch or dessert it's nice to offer your guests coffee, along with sugar and cream. A variety of juice, soda and bottled water is also a good idea, just to make sure you're covered. For an informal co-ed baby shower beer will probably be expected and appreciated.

3. Delegate Tasks as Needed

Even the most efficient Type-A personality needs help sometimes. Throwing a baby shower, especially if you're dealing with a large guest list, can be a very involved, time-consuming task. Chances are the expectant mother you're throwing the shower for has other close friends or family members who would love to help with the shower. If you need help, don't look at is as weakness on your part, but rather a way for the other women in the life of the soon-to-be mom to show her how much they love her, and how excited they are about the new baby.

One way to make baby shower planning more manageable is to ask someone to help you co-host the shower. This means that the various tasks as well as the expense of the baby shower can be divided among two or more people. The co-hosts will most likely be flattered to be asked, and happy to have a way to shower attention and love on their expecting friend or family member. Just remember to have a discussion with your co-hosts about details like the budget and how elaborate or simple the shower will be, to make sure you're all on the same page, and to avoid hard feelings later.

If you'd rather host the shower yourself or don't know any good candidates for co-hosting, you can help by simply delegating baby shower tasks. If you keep the tasks small enough, no one will be able to say no. You can just delegate easy tasks, or delegate tasks based on the specific talents and interests of the people you're asking to help.

Here are a few things you may consider delegating:

- Picking up napkins, streamers, plates, balloons, or any other miscellaneous items left on your shopping list.

- Bringing a favorite dish or dessert.

- Pitching in and purchasing a bottle or two of champagne.

- Baking and/or decorating the cake, especially if one of the guests happens to be known for her cake baking or decorating skills.

- Making a hand-made banner or table runner, if one of the guests loves to sew.

- Designing the invitations, if one of the guests happens to be a graphic designer.

- Being in charge of the RSVPs

- Getting props, pens and paper, prizes and instructions ready for any baby shower games

4. Plan Games and Activities

In addition to eating, drinking, mingling, and watching the soon-to-be mommy open her gifts, your baby shower guests will probably expect entertainment in the form of games or other activities. Baby shower games run the gamut from traditional to more off-the-wall, but whichever games you choose they are guaranteed to make your baby shower more lively and fun.

Many baby shower games have a winner, and having extra party favors or prizes on hand to give to the winners is a nice touch. Gift cards to popular retailers like Starbucks, Target or Amazon in small denominations make for easy but much appreciated prizes.

Here is a list of fun baby shower games you can refer to when planning your shower:

Baby Shower Bingo

You can buy baby shower themed Bingo cards at many party stores, or download and print a free template from the internet. Other than the cards, all you need are enough pens for everyone and a small favor or prize for every round you play. The squares on the Bingo cards can be filled in with items from the mom-to-be's gift registry, such as onesies, a stroller, sippy cups, etc. Just make sure to make each card slightly different. As she opens the gifts your guests can cross off the appropriate squares on their Bingo card until someone wins.

This game is a great way to keep the guests entertained and in a fun, competitive spirit while the mom-to-be opens her gifts, since this part of the shower can sometimes go on for quite a while. It also takes some of the attention of the mom-to-be, which is nice if she is uncomfortable being the center of attention.

Guess the Baby Food

This one will have everyone laughing. Simply set up stations with opened baby food jars in different flavors, with the labels removed, and spoons. The guests take turn having a little taste of each baby food and attempt to correctly guess the flavor. Whoever guesses the most correctly wins a prize!

Name That Tune - Baby Style

Make a mix CD or set up an iPod playlist with a variety of songs all featuring the word "baby" in the title. Pass out paper and pens to all of your guests. Designate someone to be in charge of pressing play on the CD or playlist and have them play just the first five seconds or so of each song, while your guests scramble to guess the song and write it down. Once you've gone through the whole playlist, whoever has the most correct answers wins!

Bottle Chugging

For this game you will need enough baby bottles for the number of guests, and plenty of each guest's beverage of choice. Fill the bottles with whichever beverage you want to use, whether water, juice, milk, soda, or even beer for a co-ed shower. Count to 3 and yell "chug!" Everyone then "chugs" their drink, which presents an amusing challenge since the baby bottle nipple slows things down a bit. Whoever drinks their entire bottle first wins.

Guess the Baby

This is a sweet game that will have everyone feeling nostalgic. When you send out your baby shower invitations, include a short note asking your guests to bring a picture of themselves when they were a baby. As they arrive at the shower, grab the baby pictures and hang them on a wall along with a Post-it note assigning each picture a number. Pass out pens and papers and have everyone guess which picture is of which guest. They can simply make a numbered list using the numbers assigned to each picture. Whoever guesses the most baby pictures correctly wins.

Sketch Artists

For this game, you will need enough paper plates and colored markers for everyone. This is a drawing contest, where each guest quickly sketches a picture of a baby on their paper plate and then everyone votes for the winner. To make the game super entertaining, each guest must place their paper plate on top of their head while sketching. Both the sight of everyone trying to draw a picture on top of their heads and the finished products are guaranteed to get plenty of laughs.

Diaper Derby

Here's another funny one that doesn't require expensive props. All you will need is a few rolls of toilet paper and a timer. Divide your guests into small teams and hand each team a roll of toilet paper. Each team has to select one member to be the "baby." The team then has one or two minutes (use a timer) to wrap the toilet paper around the grown "baby" as a diaper, being as creative as possible.

Bobbing for Nipples

This is a silly game that will bring out your guests' competitive sides. You will need several large plastic buckets as well as lots of plastic baby bottle nipples. If you'd rather not use nipples you can use small plastic babies or anything small, plastic and baby-related. Simply line up the buckets, fill them with water and add several of the nipples or other items to each bucket. Your guests will line up behind a bucket, standing on their knees with their hands behind their backs. On the count of three they will start bobbing for nipples, spitting them out on the ground as they find them with their mouths. The first guest to get all the items in their bucket wins.

Pin the Baby on the Mom

This game is a baby shower version of the classic children's birthday party game, Pin the Tail on the Donkey. Just like in Pin the Tail on the Donkey, when kids pin a tail on a big paper donkey while blindfolded, in this game your blindfolded baby shower guests will tape a paper cutout baby on the expectant mom. The goal is to tape the baby as close to the mom's tummy as possible without being able to see what they're doing. Whoever gets the baby closest to the pregnant belly wins the game. For his one you will need tape, a pre-made cutout of a paper baby, and a blindfold.

Spit the Pacifier

For this game, you will need as many pacifiers as you have baby shower guests. You will line up your baby shower guests and give them each a pacifier to place in their mouth. They will each spit the pacifier as far as they can, and the one who gets theirs the farthest wins.

Baby-Changing Relay

This is a fast-paced, active baby shower game. For this game you will need dolls that you dress ahead of time in a diaper and baby clothes and then swaddle in a baby blanket. You will also need three prizes. You will divide your guests into teams of three and have them lined up at long tables, in stations. When you yell "Go!" or count down from 3, the first person on each team unwraps the baby blanket as quickly as they can and passes the baby doll to the next person on their team. That person will undress the doll and pass it to the next person. The next person will change the doll's diaper and pass it back. Next the middle team member re-dresses the doll and passes it back to the first person on the team, who re-swaddles the doll in the blanket. Whichever team gets through all the steps the quickest wins.

Guess the Baby Items

For this game, you will need a diaper bag or cloth tote bag as well as 10-15 practical, inexpensive baby items that you will place in the bag. You will also need enough pens and paper for every guest. Some good items to include in the bag are a bottle, a pacifier, a diaper, a bib, a plush toy, a onesie, a teething ring, a rattle, etc. Pass out the pens and paper and then begin to pass the bag of baby items around. Each guest gets a minute or two to rifle around in the bag without looking inside and write down all of their guesses for the items in the bag. Once all of your guests get a chance to make their guesses, whoever guesses the most correct items wins the game (and a prize).

Celebrity Baby Name

This is a fun game for any pop culture enthusiasts attending your baby shower. It doesn't require any props, though it does require some preparation. Before the baby shower invest some time doing internet research into celebrity's baby names. Compile a list including a good mixture of bizarre (like actor Jason Lee's baby Pilot Inspektor or Gwyneth Paltrow's daughter Apple) and more common baby names. As you read through the baby names list your guests will shout out their guesses. Move on to the next name after someone guesses correctly. This game is just for fun and no prizes are needed.

Money Talk

For this game, you will need a piggy bank, and a list of "Have you ever?" questions (can easily be found online. You will also need to let your guests know to bring any spare change that they have with them. Depending on the crowd you can make the "Have you ever?" questions really innocent or a little risqué. Set the piggy bank in the middle of the room and make sure your shower guests have their change ready. Read one question at a time and if anyone's answer to the question is "yes," they will walk up to the piggy bank and drop in a coin. This game is fun because it serves as an ice breaker, letting the baby shower guests get to know each other better. It had the added benefit of providing the parents-to-be with a gift of a new piggy bank full of change- baby's first savings account!

Memory Game

For this fun memory game, you will need a clothesline with clips, pens and paper, and miscellaneous baby items that can be easily clipped to the clothesline. Some ideas for items include onesies, swaddling blankets, bibs, and items like rattles and pacifiers that can be hung up with ribbon or string. Before the guests arrive you will hang up the items in a random order, and make sure to jot down the list of items in the order in which they're hanging up. The guests will all be given a pen and paper and will have 30 seconds or so to stare at the clothesline and attempt to memorize the items. Then you take them all down and the guests write the items down in the order they think they were strung up. Anyone gets all of the items in the correct order wins.

The Poopy Diaper Game

For the parents to be, poopy diapers will soon be a major part of everyday life. This game plays around with the idea of poopy diapers in a way that is much more pleasant than the real thing. For this game you'll need several poopy diapers along with the same number of different chocolate bars (Snicker's, Kit Kat, Twix, etc.) You will melt the chocolate bars one at a time and place the melted chocolate in a diaper making it look "poopy," and making a note of which diaper contains which chocolate bar. Your shower guests will then take turns tasting the different chocolate and guess the candy bars. Whoever guesses the most correctly wins.

Baby Price is Right

For this game, you will need to purchase some things ahead of time. Purchase a large basket along with several affordable baby items. Some options include a onesie, a bottle, a rattle, a tube of diaper cream, and a stuffed plush toy for baby. Before removing the price tags make sure to tally up your receipts and write down the total cost of the basket and all of the items in a secret place where no one will see it. Set the basket in the center of the room where everyone can have a chance to look at all of the items. Have your guests guess the total cost of the basket and all the included items, and jot down their guess on a scrap of paper. Whoever's guess is the closest to the cost of the basket and items wins a small game prize. The best part of this game is that the parents-to-be get to keep the basket along with all the practical objects inside.

Baby Word Jumble

This is a fun game for any baby shower guests who are fans of word games. Before the baby shower you will need to make (or find on the internet) a list of common baby words, but with the spelling jumbled. For example, "rattle" could become "lettra." Make sure to make enough copies of the word jumble for all of your guests to have their own, and pass them out along with pens. The first guest to correctly un-jumble all the words wins!

Guess the Mom-to-Be's Belly Measurements

This game involves having some fun with your pregnant guest of honor's ever-expanding baby bump. All you need for this game is a large ball of string or yarn and a pair of scissors. Pass around the yarn or string and scissors and have the baby shower guests take their best guess of how big the mom-to-be's belly is. They will simply cut the string as long as they think they should and pass along the scissors to the next guest. Once everyone has their string or yarn cut, they can take turns going up to the soon-to-be mommy and trying out their string by wrapping it around her waist. Whoever's measurement is the closest wins!

Write a Book Together

This isn't technically a game, but rather a fun and thoughtful activity that will provide the parents-to-be with a beloved keepsake from their baby shower. Purchase a large blank book, preferably one with a cover that references babies in some way or fits with your baby shower theme. Set out the book along with several pens. You can also leave a short note with instructions. Encourage your guests to write down thoughts and well wishes for the parents-to-be. Some great things to include are advice for new parents (especially if many of the other baby shower guests are already parents), well wishes, blessings, funny jokes about babies, and any other thoughts that come to mind. This blank book gives the baby shower guests something to do other than play games, and doubles as a thoughtful present for the new parents.

Perform a Ritual

This activity will work best at very small and intimate baby showers where the guests know each other well, especially if the mother-to-be and other guests are of a spiritual or religious bent. As a party favor, you can give each of the guests their own candle. When you are ready for the special ritual, simply gather around a table with your candles and a lighter or matches. One at a time, each guest will light their candle and then say a blessing, prayer, or positive intention for the new baby. This can be a very powerful and moving moment in a baby shower, but will probably not work as well for a larger crowd, or a rowdier, more humorous baby shower event.

5. Don't Forget the Favors and Prizes

Party favors and prizes are another baby shower detail you will probably want to take care of ahead of time. These can be store-bought or handmade, simple or labor-intensive, very inexpensive or more on the pricy side. It's really up to your own preferences and budget (and those of any co-hostesses who are helping you with the shower). At a minimum you will probably want one nice party favor per guest which will give them something thoughtful to take home after the shower, and a variety of simple prizes for any games you have planned. Here are some favor ideas to get you started:

Gift Cards

Everyone loves to get a gift card. You can get a bunch of them in small denominations (say $5) to a variety of shops or websites to use as prizes. Gift cards for coffee shops, bookstores, online retailers and spas are always extra popular.

Lip balm

Either buy them or make them at home in cute tins (there are tons of easy-to-follow tutorials available online). A nice touch is to make or order customized labels in the baby shower color scheme with the mom and/or baby's name and the date of the shower.

Flowers

Fresh flowers are always a thoughtful gesture. An affordable way to give all of your guests fresh flowers as a party favor is to decorate with small, vintage or vintage-inspired bud vases each holding a single stem or two of a beautiful flower. The flowers and vases can be chosen in colors that complement your baby shower theme and color scheme. Hydrangeas, tulips and daffodils are especially popular.

Baby Bottles Filled with M&Ms

You can buy small plastic baby bottles in assorted colors quite inexpensively. Fill with M&Ms and you have an affordable, colorful, baby-themed favor that will satisfy your guests' sweet tooth.

Small Potted Succulents

Succulents are visually appealing and low-maintenance: a great combination! You can pick up simple pots matching your color scheme and plant them before the shower. Even your baby shower guests with a major brown thumb will be able to appreciate these easy to care for houseplants!

Lollipops

There is something so sweet and retro about a brightly colored lollipop tied with ribbon. Best of all, they come in a wide range of colors, require no real set-up, and are super affordable!

Candy Wrapped in Tulle

For a classic baby shower favor, try wrapping Jordan almonds or other small candies in tulle and tie with a ribbon. These look extra pretty sitting in the middle of each guest's plate at a nicely made-up table.

Bun in the Oven

Here's another cute party favor idea to satisfy your guests' sweet tooth. This party favor idea is a play on the phrase "bun in the oven" which is a cute way to say that someone is expecting a baby. The mom-to-be of course has a "bun in the oven," but with these party favors so can the baby shower guests. Simply make or buy a big batch of delicious sticky buns or cinnamon rolls ahead of time. Individually wrap the sweet treats in cellophane or in their own classic white bakery boxes (these come in all different sizes, so you should be able to find one that is perfect for cinnamon rolls). You can add a cute label in your baby shower colors that says something like "Enjoy your own sweet 'bun in the oven!'"

Individually-wrapped Soaps or Small Bottles of Lotion

After taking the time to shower the mom-to-be with love, attention, and gifts, let your baby shower guests know they should indulge themselves a little too. A thoughtful bath and body gift is always a hit and they come in a wide array of scents and packaging.

Homemade Baked Yumminess

If you or a co-hostess love to bake, this is the delicious, budget-friendly favor for you.

Simply bake a batch of cupcakes, macarons or sugar cookies decorated in your baby shower colors. Wrap in cellophane and tie with a pretty ribbon, or box up in a small bakery box decorated with a customized label. Your guests will love this one.

Candles

Everyone loves a deliciously scented candle. Best of all, candles can easily be customized with handmade labels.

Personalized Mints

Small metal tubs of mints make cute, inexpensive favors. You can purchase them wholesale with customized labels from many online party stores without spending a ton of money.

Chapter 3: Hosting Your Baby Shower

If you've been following this baby shower guide so far, you should have the preparation stage totally under control. This means you should have tackled the guest list, sent out invitations, tracked all of your RSVPs (and wrangle responses from anyone you didn't hear from), decided on a theme and/or color scheme, planned fun games, planned a delicious menu, and purchased or made all of the decorations and favors you need. Whew- great job! Hopefully you also followed our advice to delegate a few of those tasks, and are feeling relaxed, stress-free, and excited for the day of the baby shower.

Here's everything you need to handle the actual day-of events and be the baby shower "hostess with the mostest!"

1. Get the Food and Drinks Ready

In order to minimize stress on the day of the shower and maximize your time with your guests, you will want to get as much of the food and drinks ready the day before as possible. Depending on what you're serving you may be able to make most of the food the night before, cover with plastic wrap or tin foil, refrigerate overnight, and then in the morning simply heat up in the oven any food that you are serving warm.

In cases where the food will taste much better if cooked right before the shower, you can still save time by prepping all of the ingredients the night before. Chopping veggies, placing fruit on skewers, slicing meats and cheeses, etc., can add up to be quite time-consuming so it's best to get these tasks out of the way ahead of time.

Another way to save time is to set the table the night before. Get out your nice dishes, glassware, silverware and cloth napkins. Arrange the table (or stack plates on a countertop if you are planning a buffet) and see how things look. Doing this the night before gives you time to get it just right, whereas right before the baby shower you will likely be in way too much of a hurry.

If you are picking up any pre-prepared food items, whether from a grocery store, bakery or even a friend's house, try to do so the day before if possible. If you need to pick things up the day of consider delegating this task to a co-hostess or friend.

In the hour or so before your guests arrive you can start getting things out of the fridge or oven, arrange them on platters and serving dishes (which you can also get ready the night before) and set out on display. Mix together the punch ingredients and ice if you are serving punch. Make sure that all of the dishes have serving utensils to go with them. Set out glassware, not just at the table, but in the kitchen or wherever you will be offering beverages before sitting down to eat. If serving champagne, get the flutes ready, perhaps on a nice tray. Having fresh raspberries on hand to drop into each champagne glass is a classy touch.

2. Setting up the Decorations and Games

Since your decorations are most likely non-perishable (and even flowers can be arranged a little ahead of time), there is no reason to procrastinate on setting them up, at least if you are throwing the baby shower at home. If you've stayed organized in your baby shower planning your decorations are most likely already assembled and stashed neatly somewhere you can get to quickly and easily. Now is the time to take them out and arrange them.

Blow up any balloons and tie them together in bunches or attach a single balloon to each chair. Hang any banners, bunting or celebratory signs that you have. Find cute ways to set up the favors and prizes, perhaps on the guests' plates at the table, or grouped together on cute decorative trays. Set out any candles you plan to use for decorations and make sure to have lighters or matches close by.

Flowers should wait until as close to the baby shower as possible in order to preserve their freshness, but they can be purchased the night before and kept overnight in cold water. This will give you a chance to arrange them ahead of time. Streamers can of course be hung up ahead of time as well.

Depending on how involved o complicated your decorations are, arranging the decorations can be quite time-consuming, so this is a great task to ask friends to come over and help with the night before the baby shower.

If you are hosting the baby shower at a location other than your home, such as a public park, church hall, or private room at a restaurant, you will need to find out from the events manager when you will have access to the location in order to set up the decorations. In most cases you won't have access to the site until an hour or so before the shower, in which case you should keep the decorations more on the simple side and definitely enlist some help. Do what you can at home the night before, such as blowing up balloons and arranging flowers, which you can transport by vehicle the next day in boxes or bins.

You can also set up the games the night before, or even earlier than that. Simply gather all of the props you need for the specific games you plan to play. To keep things neat and uncluttered you can set the props aside in cute decorative baskets. Just make sure to keep them in the room or area where you plan to play the games, in order to keep the day of the shower as streamlined as possible.

By the time of the baby shower, the house or other location should already be decorated and ready to go. When you get to the games portion of the baby shower, simply make an announcement that you are ready to play a few games, and start passing out the props while explaining the directions. Luckily, all of the game ideas in this guide have easy to explain rules and uncomplicated props.

3. Arrange the Seating

Keep in mind that your baby shower probably requires a couple of different seating areas: one for mingling and eating and one for gathering around the mom-to-be and watching her open her gifts. If you happen to have enough chairs (or are willing to rent or borrow some) for each guest to have two seats, this will be no problem. Simply set up chairs either at the dining room table (for a sit-down meal) or scattered around your house in social seating groups if you are serving a buffet and encouraging your guests to sit wherever they'd like during the meal. Then arrange the rest of the chairs in a semi-circle fashion in the living or sitting room so that your guests will be able to watch the guest of honor open her baby gifts.

If you only have enough chairs for everyone to have one, don't worry. Simply ask a few friends to help you quickly move the chairs from the dining area to the gift-opening area after everyone eats. With help this should only take a few minutes and be pretty unobtrusive.

If you are hosting your shower at a restaurant or bar someone will probably be on hand to arrange the chairs for you. Just make sure to let the manager or event planner know ahead of time if you have specific preferences, and also be sure to give them a head count. If you are having the shower at a park, you will probably be using picnic tables, but may also want to bring chairs from home or rent them from the park and arrange them before your guests arrive.

4. Taking Photos

Ideally you will be able to delegate photography to another guest or a co-hostess. You will likely be busy with various aspects of hosting the baby shower and will therefore miss a lot of the best photo opportunities. If any of the guests happens to be a great photographer, ask them if they would mind taking a handful of photos during the shower. If not, just mention to multiple guests that you are hoping to have some nice photo mementos for the mom-to-be after the shower, and ask them to bring their cameras if they don't mind. If several people are taking pictures, even if none of them are especially good at photography you should have plenty of decent pictures after the event.

After the party you can always set up an account on a photo sharing site for everyone to upload their baby shower photos. You can email the link to your guests. This way the mom-to-be can take her pick of which photos she would like to save, upload to Facebook, or print. If you really want to go above and beyond, you can save the best ones to your own computer, lightly edit them if you know how to do so, and then order a photo book online. This will make a thoughtful gift for the mom-to-be, helping her to remember the beautiful baby shower you threw for her.

While the mom-to-be will most likely want photos to remember the day, it's also worth mentioning that you shouldn't go too overboard with photography. She may not want a camera flash going off in her face every time she opens a present, and if you or your guests spend the whole event taking pictures you may not have time to be in the moment and enjoy yourselves. A handful of photos from select moments throughout the shower should be more than sufficient.

5. Etiquette Reminders

We can all use a few gentle etiquette reminders when hosting a baby shower or other social event. Here are a few things to keep in mind as the baby shower hostess:

- **Be mindful of any guests for whom a baby shower may be a difficult or sensitive event.** For example, perhaps one of your guests is known to be struggling with infertility or has even lost a baby. A celebration focused on the excitement of a new baby may be emotionally difficult for a guest in this situation. This doesn't mean that you shouldn't invite them, of course, but rather that you should be sensitive to their feelings.

Before sending out the invitation, you or the mom-to-be should call the guest and gently ask them if they are up to it. If they say that they are, go ahead and send an invitation, but find a delicate way to broach the subject before the baby shower, just checking in with them to see how they feel and if there's anything you can do to make them feel more comfortable. Then, on the day of the actual shower, you can check in with them a few times, but still allowing them their space. Be there for them if they need to talk quietly in private, and don't make a big deal of it if they decide to leave early.

- **Set your shyness aside.** Even if you're not normally especially outgoing or sociable, in offering to host a baby shower you've taken responsibility for keeping the party lively, light-hearted and fun. This means mingling, starting conversations, introducing guests who don't already know each other, and generally being the life of the party in any way that you can.

- **Cut off the alcohol.** If you are serving champagne or other alcoholic beverages, as hostess it is your duty to make sure that no one over-indulges and then gets into a potentially serious situation. Limit the amount of alcohol to a couple of drinks per guest, and/or stop serving alcohol an hour or so before the party ends. If you are worried about any of your guests having a bit too much to drink at the shower, it may be a good idea to abstain from alcohol yourself so that you will be available to act as a sober driver or to coordinate taxis or designated driver carpools for guests in need. This may be more likely to be needed if you have a co-ed baby shower, especially at a bar or in another more lively environment.

- **Be present in the moment.** Hosting a baby shower involves a lot of details that can easily keep you occupied throughout the day. Just remember the reason that you're hosting the shower in the first place is to honor and demonstrate your love for a close friend or family member. She will most likely

want to see that you're enjoying yourself and have time to talk to her and the
other guests, instead of hustling
through one activity or task after another. This is another great reason to
organize and plan the shower as much
as possible ahead of time, and also to
consider delegating some of the tasks.

- **Keep an eye on plates and glasses.** As
  the baby shower hostess, it is up to you
  to make sure your guests are well-fed
  and don't go thirsty. If you notice
  someone walking around with an emp-
  ty plate or glass offer them a refill right
  away. Depending on the set-up you can
  also encourage guests to "help themselves" to seconds and drink refills.

- **Take care of the little snags and hic-
  cups yourself.** Even the best-planned
  baby shower will likely face small challenges and snags. Maybe you will run
  out of ice, or that camera you checked
  for fresh batteries will stop working for
  no apparent reason just as you start to
  take pictures. Whatever it is, don't
  sweat the small stuff, and most importantly do what you can to keep

these little issues from the mom-to-be's attention. Let her relax and bask in the attention and love she's receiving, without worrying about problems that come up. Of course, the more organized and carefully planned the baby shower, the less likely these little problems and issues are to pop up.

- **Don't forget to say thank you.** Don't get so caught up in the busy day that you forget your manners. Even though you've possibly done the majority of the work in hosting the baby shower, the guests have also taken time out of their busy schedules in order to attend. A good hostess always thanks her guests for coming, thanks them throughout the baby shower for any extra help they offer you (for example, with setting out food, taking pictures, keeping track of the gifts, etc.), and then thanks them again as they are leaving. Your guests will feel so taken care of and appreciated, they won't even notice any little things that happen to go wrong.

6. Keeping Track of Gifts

Either you as the hostess or someone that you designate to help should be in charge of keeping track of the gifts as the mom-to-be opens them. Simply keep a notebook or piece of paper and a good pen (with a couple of back-ups) on hand in the gift area. As the mom-to-be opens the gifts write them down along with the name of whoever the gift is from. If you miss a name, make sure to ask the mom-to-be to repeat it and be sure to write it down before she moves on to opening the next gift.

After the gifts have all been opened and the cards start to get scattered and mixed up it can be next to impossible to figure out who gave which gift, so keeping this list organized and accurate is very important. If it's a larger baby shower with a whole lot of presents, you might want to assign a few different helpers for this task, to prevent it from growing too tedious for one person. After all of the gifts have been opened, be sure to set the gift list aside in a safe place where it won't be accidentally thrown away.

Sometime in the day or two after the baby shower, make sure to get the gift list to the mom-to-be. If you have the time to do this, an extra thoughtful gesture would be to type up the list of gifts with the givers' names along with their addresses, which you should already have from when you mailed the shower invitations. This will help the mom-to-be send out her thank you cards promptly and without stress, and will also eliminate any confusion caused by hard-to-read handwriting on the handwritten list. Or, you can simply skip this step and type the original list while the mom-to-be is opening her shower gifts. This will work if you're comfortable having your laptop computer or tablet device out at the baby shower.

Chapter 4: Baby Shower Timeline

This handy timeline is just a suggestion and can be customized or changed as you see fit. This is a timeline for the events of the actual baby shower. A typical baby shower lasts 2-3 hours.

- **Guests arrive.** Personally greet each guest as they come in, to make them feel comfortable and welcome. Offer to take their coats, show them where to leave gifts and cards, and then offer them a beverage and possibly an appetizer or two, depending on your menu.

- **After all of your guests have arrived, say a few words honoring the mom-to-be.** Get everyone's attention, perhaps by dinging your champagne glass with a fork as though you're going to give a toast. Welcome everyone to the baby shower and thank them for coming.

Remind everyone that you're here to celebrate the mom-to-be and her new baby. Say a few kind words about the mom-to-be, and if she is comfortable with this and you've discussed it ahead of time, let her say a few things as well. She might want the chance to quickly thank everyone for coming and you for hosting the baby shower.

- **Let your guests start to mingle and make introductions.** If you notice that any guests don't know each other, introduce them to each other and then move along to the next group of guests, allowing people to make conversation with each other. Be especially mindful of any guests who seem shy or who don't know many people at the shower.

- **Make sure that everyone has a drink** and start offering snacks or appetizers and passing them around, if you haven't already done so.

- **Now is the time to play games.** Get the game props ready, get everyone's attention, and explain the rules. Pass out props and divide the guests into teams as needed. Pass out prizes to the winners.

- **It's time to eat!** Depending on your menu and the type of shower you're having, either ask everyone to have a seat and then beginning serving the food, or have them line up at the buffet and grab plates, silverware, drinks and food. Serve cake and champagne or punch afterward, or skip straight ahead to the dessert if you're having a dessert-only baby shower.

- **Quickly clear the dishes in an unobtrusive manner.** Don't worry about the dirty dishes yet. They can wait until after the baby shower is over. If you start doing dishes in the middle of the party guests will feel guilty and like they need to help. Simply clear the dirty dishes and neatly stack them out of sight in the sink or on a counter, and then move on with the party.

- **Time for the main event - the presents!** Now that everyone has mingled, had a blast playing games, and enjoyed your delicious food and drinks, it's time to "shower" the honored guest with presents. Gather everyone around (you should have chairs already arranged in the gift-opening area), get your pen and paper ready to keep track of the gifts (or give the pen and paper to your helper), and encourage the mom-to-be to start opening gifts. You can stack presents near her chair or simply hand them to her as she goes. Get ready for lots of excited "Ooohs" and "Ahhhs!" After the gifts are opened, quickly grab a trash bag and throw away the discarded gift wrap.

- **Wind-down time.** Now it's time for your party to gradually come to an end. Don't make any abrupt announcements about the baby shower being over, but rather allow guests to continue to mingle, snack, have a second slice of cake, congratulate the expectant mommy, etc. They will start to gradually leave of their own accord. As you say your goodbyes, be sure to offer each guest their parting party favor. Just as you greeted each guest as they arrived, be sure to personally say goodbye to everyone and thank them so much for coming.

- **Give the mom-to-be a big hug good-bye** and help her load her baby gifts into her car. She shouldn't be carting away heavy gifts when she's pregnant, so make sure she has help at home with getting the gifts inside. She will be glowing with happiness after being showered with love, attention, well wishes and gifts all day- and it's all thanks to you!

- **Take off your shoes and relax for a bit before you start the clean-up.** You just pulled off hosting an amazing baby shower! Pat yourself on the back and relax with an extra slice of cake or glass of champagne, knowing that you did a great job and helped the mom-to-be feel loved and special.

- **Clean-up.** After all your hard work, you may want to consider enlisting the help of family members or friends to make cleaning up less time-consuming. If you had the shower at home you will of course have plenty of dishes to wash, decorations to put away and chairs and tables to rearrange. If you have the shower at a park or other public place you will probably have a limited amount of time to tear down. On the other hand, if your shower was held at a restaurant or bar the staff will probably handle this aspect of the baby shower for you.

Chapter 5: Handy Step-by-step Checklist

Now that you know everything you need to know about hosting the perfect baby shower, here is a handy checklist to use. Simply go down the list and check items off as you complete them, and your baby shower will be exquisitely planned and flawlessly executed in no time at all.

Two-three Months Before

- Decide who is hosting the shower. Are you hosting alone or will you have co-hosts?

- With the in-put of the mother-to-be, determine the overall feel or mood you want to create for the baby shower.

Casual or formal? Dressy brunch or laidback BBQ? Co-ed or ladies only?

- Decide on a budget. If you are co-hosting the shower you will of course need to decide on a budget that all of the hosts are comfortable with.

- With the help of the guest of honor, make and finalize the guest list and collect addresses for the invitations.

- Decide on a date for the baby shower. Make sure to double-check for any potential schedule conflicts with any guests who are particularly important with the mother-to-be, such as her immediate family or best friend. Don't schedule the baby shower too close to a family wedding or graduation, for example.

- Decide on the location. Would you prefer to host the shower in your own home, or elsewhere, like at a public park, in a church, or in a private room of a restaurant or bar?

One Month Before

- Decide on the theme.

- Select or design and mail the baby shower invitations. Be sure to include directions to the

- Order or make the baby shower invitations. Be sure to include the baby shower location, registry information, and any special game instructions (for example if you choose a game that requires guests to bring an item from home).

- Address, stamp and mail the invitations. If you're sending e-vites, send them now. Plan the menu, including who is bringing what if you plan to ask anyone else to bring dishes.

- Make a general plan the decorations, including color scheme. Will you have fresh flowers, balloons, streamers, banners, a centerpiece etc.? Make a list.

- Begin getting ideas for the games you'd like to play and jot them down.

Three-Four Weeks Before

- Order the cake if you aren't planning to make it yourself. If you are planning to make it yourself decide on a recipe and how you are going to decorate the cake.

- Order flowers if you plan to get them from a florist.

- Order chairs if you need to rent them. Decide or finalize which games you would like played at the shower and make a list of props that you will need.

- Make an overall baby shower shopping list including any decorations, favors, game props, food and drinks that you have to purchase.

Two Weeks Before

- Buy or make all of the decorations, party favors, and game prizes.

- Buy any plates, glassware, cups, napkins, tablecloths, and eating utensils needed if you are going to host the baby shower at home and not planning to use your own items.

- Finalize the menu and seating set-up with the restaurant or bar if you are hosting your shower there

One Week Before

- Finalize the guests head count.

- Call those who have not RSVP'd to get their response.

- Wrap, decorate, or otherwise arrange the party favors and game prizes.

- If you're planning to use your camera double check that it has fresh batteries, and purchase extra if needed.

- If the shower is at your home, give the house an extra good cleaning the week before the shower.

- Customize our baby shower day-of timeline (in the next section) for your baby shower and print a copy.

- Buy your gift for mommy-to-be from her registry and wrap it. Wrapping it in a way that complements the baby shower theme or color scheme is a nice, thoughtful touch.

The Day Before

- Begin setting up the decorations if you're having the shower in your home. If you're having it at an outside location set the decorations up as much as possible and get them ready to be transported.

- Set up tables & chairs if the baby shower will be hosted in your home.

- Buy all food and drink items and begin prepping them.

- Cook or bake anything that can be made ahead of time. Prep everything else.

- If you're getting your flowers from a grocer you can buy them the night before. Trim the stems and make your arrangements, being sure to keep the flowers in water overnight.

- Get baby shower game props and prizes organized and set up in the appropriate location.

- Bake or arrange to pick up the baby shower cake.

The Big Day!

- Get your baby shower timeline out and keep it somewhere you can see it easily. It will keep you on track throughout the day and most importantly help keep your day free of stress and chaos.

- Pick up flowers from the florist if you ordered them and didn't do so last night.

- Pick up the cake if you ordered one from a bakery.

- If you're having the shower at your home, finalize any decorations you set-up last night. If your baby shower is elsewhere bring the decorations there and set up now.

- Set out the dishes, glassware, etc., if you didn't do so last night.

- Set out the food if you're hosting the baby shower at home. Make sure there are serving utensils.

- Set out the baby shower party favors if you didn't do so last night.

- Set out the food if you're hosting the shower at home. Make sure there are serving utensils.

- As guests arrive, greet them and offer them a beverage.

- Quickly chat with anyone you've designated to take photos to remind them and make sure they brought their cameras.

- Stick with your timeline and make friendly announcements whenever you change activities, for example from mingling to eating to games to opening gifts.

- Either make notes yourself of who gave each gift, or designate someone to do so. After the baby shower you can give the mom-to-be this list along with the list of addresses you should have from sending out the baby shower invitations. This will make the thank you note process a snap for the new mom.

- Don't forget to relax and enjoy the wonderful baby shower you worked so hard to plan! Enjoy some delicious cake, laugh and chat with friends, and feel great knowing you planned a beautiful, fun day for the mom-to-be.

Chapter 6: Things to Avoid When Hosting a Baby Shower

Now that we've got you covered with all the to-dos for hosting the perfect baby shower, here are twelve don'ts to keep in mind. Avoid committing any of these baby shower faux-pas for a fun-filled, meaningful baby shower:

1. **Not picking a theme or color scheme.** While not mandatory, picking a theme or at least a simple color scheme brings everything together in an aesthetically pleasing way. If you don't settle on a theme or color scheme it's likely your baby shower will seem scattered, incohesive, and a little chaotic. You will likely also be a bit more stressed out since all of the little decisions along the way, including picking out the invitations, the decorations and games, can be made much more easily with a unifying theme to tie them all together.

2. **Not delegating tasks when you're too busy to do everything.** Even Super Woman needs help sometimes! For some of us, asking for help is really hard because we like to be seen as capable of "doing it all." Just keep in mind that the baby shower is for the mom-to-be, not just a way to show off what a great multi-tasker you are. The guest of honor will be much happier with her baby shower if she has a relaxed, happy hostess in charge of it. If you're stressed and stretched too thin, it will show and put a damper on the mood of the baby shower. Plus, asking for help is a great way to let the mom-to-be's other friends or family members feel included and welcome.

3. **Forgetting to take photos.** There's probably no need to hire a professional photographer or to capture every second of the day, but the mom-to-be will probably be a little disappointed if she has no pictures to remember the day with. To help ensure that there are plenty of pictures capturing special moments throughout the day, you will probably want to make sure that more than one person is bringing a camera. If you plan to take pictures yourself make

sure your camera has fresh batteries (or is newly charged) and plenty of memory. Some moments that the mom-to-be will likely want captured include everyone mingling and having a great time, guests playing silly games while laughing, the mom-to-be opening gifts, and a handful of posed shots of the mom-to-be with her close friends and family members.

4. **Not budgeting.** Just like any big party or event, hosting a baby shower can quickly become expensive, perhaps much more so than anticipated. Setting a specific budget at the on-set, either just for yourself or together with the co-hosts if you have any, can help keep down costs and keep your bank account from taking too much of a beating. Knowing that you have a budget will encourage you to look for discounts and other deals, and probably prevent you from splurging on too many extras that you may not be able to afford. It's absolutely possible to host a beautiful baby shower on a budget, as long as you act in an intentional manner. Here are some quick tips to save money and stay on budget when hosting a baby shower:

- Host the shower at home instead of a rented or otherwise expensive location.

- Consider an appetizers only, dessert only, or cake and punch reception instead of serving a full meal. Just make sure to mention this on the invitation and try to avoid having the shower around lunch or dinner time.

- Make the food and bake the cake yourself, or enlist the help of any talented cooks and chefs in your family.

- Simplify the decorations and favors. Streamers, balloons and simple favors such as mints or Jordan almonds are all beloved classics that happen to be inexpensive.

- Keep the guest list small and under control. The more guests you invite, the more food, drinks, game prizes and party favors you have to purchase.

- Co-host the shower with one or more friend or family member of the mom-to-be. Co-hosting lets the expense be spread out more and divided among a

few people, instead of all being shoul-
dered by a single hostess.

5. **Playing Embarrassing or Off-Color Games.** If you're having a very casual, co-ed baby shower with a younger crowd, you may be able to get away with this, but in general games should be kept light-hearted and G-rated. Just remember, this is a baby shower celebrating new mother-hood, not a wild college party or bache-lorette party. Keep the games and activities especially mild and innocent if any elderly female relatives or friends of the mom-to-be are invited.

6. **Not having enough food or drinks.** There are tons of ways to save money when throwing a baby shower. Skimping on the amount of food and drinks you offer shouldn't be one of them. Nothing is worse than sitting through a party with a grumbling stomach because there wasn't enough food to go around, and you will definitely not want to miss a chunk of the baby shower because you had to run to the grocery store to pick up extra snacks or drinks. It's probably best to err on the side of having too much food and drinks, just in

case. You can always send guests home with leftovers if you need to.

7. **Procrastinating.** We're all prone to procrastination now and again, but if throwing a fun, low-stress baby shower is your goal procrastination is your enemy. If you follow our baby shower guide, and stick to our checklist, you will glide through the baby shower planning process with grace and no stress. If on the other hand, you wait until the last minute you will give yourself many sleepless, worried nights and throw a baby shower that is less wonderful than it could be. For your own mental health and the sake of throwing a great baby shower, get started on your planning as soon as possible, without unnecessary delays. Break up the bigger or more daunting tasks into smaller ones that you can do gradually over the course of weeks or months leading up to the shower.

8. **Serving food lots of people are allergic to without double-checking with your guests first.** Some of the most common food allergies include shellfish, peanuts and dairy. You have a few options for handling possible food allergens. The goal

is to be able to serve the food you want to, without risking any of your guests becoming sick or going hungry. One way to approach this is to include a short note on your invitations asking guests to please mention any dietary restrictions or food allergies when they RSVP. Then, if no one mentions any when calling to RSVP, you can feel free to serve whatever food you wish. Another option is to just serve a large enough variety of food that everyone, including vegetarians and those with food allergies, can find something to eat. You can even go the extra mile and create cute labels for each dish which list the main ingredients, if you wish to do so.

9. **Letting stress or a bad mood ruin the day.** As the baby shower hostess, part of your role is to remain gracious, kind, light-hearted and polite throughout the day, regardless of how you feel inside or what is going on in your life. Maybe you're having a bad week, experiencing personal problems, or just stressed out about the baby shower itself. Regardless, you will need to set these feelings aside and put on a happy, gracious face. It is unfair to the mom-

to-be and the other guests to take out your bad mood on them, and a stressed out or short-tempered hostess can easily ruin an otherwise lovely baby shower. If you are concerned that this may be a problem, build some stress-busters into your week before the baby shower. Get a massage, take a gentle yoga class, do some deep breathing exercises, or simply end the day with a bubble bath and a glass of wine.

10. **Cleaning up while everyone is still having fun.** If you're hosting the baby shower in your own home, and especially if you are something of a "neat freak," those piles of dirty dishes and glasses may start to bother you long before the shower is over. Just do what you can to ignore the mess until your guests leave, however. Quickly clearing the plates and grabbing discarded wrapping paper from the floor is fine, but more thorough cleaning while your guests are still present can be seen as rude. If your guests are still hanging out, chatting, and enjoying themselves, the sight of the party hostess scrubbing dishes or mopping the floor will only make them uncomfortable. Cleaning signals to your guests that

they've overstayed their welcome, which is not a message a gracious, polite hostess wants to send. Relax and enjoy your guests and the mother-to-be's company for a while. The dishes will still be there after the baby shower has officially ended.

11. **Not cleaning at all.** Maybe you are one of those laidback souls who never notices towels piled on the bathroom floor or a thick layer of dust on the dining room table, well, if you're hosting the baby shower in your own home, you will need to temporarily be more conscientious about these things. Thoroughly clean your home the week before you host the baby shower (enlist help, paid or otherwise, if you really hate to clean). Then, just before guests arrive do a quick walk-through your home. Any clutter, including stacks of mail or visible dirty laundry, should be quickly put away. If you have to, shove everything into an out of the way closest until after the party. You want your guests to notice the glowing mom-to-be and your tasteful decorations, not your messy house.

12. **Inviting too many people.** If you want to throw your baby shower in a smaller

space, whether a home, private room at a restaurant, or elsewhere, be careful not to invite more guests than you have room for. An otherwise fun baby shower can quickly feel cramped and claustrophobic if too many guests are crammed into a small space together. Inviting too many guests may also mean not having enough seating, or even worse, food and drinks for everyone in attendance. If your guest list has gotten out of control and you're nervously eyeing your smaller home, consider hosting the shower in a bigger space, like a public park or church hall, instead.

Conclusion

Congratulations! If you've followed all the helpful steps and advice in our baby shower guide, you are well on your way to hosting the ultimate baby shower. By now you know how to select the perfect baby shower theme, plan unique and creative decorations, and send great, eye-catching invitations. You also know how to plan a delicious, palate-pleasing menu, as well as fun games that will have your guests laughing hysterically. You've got baby shower etiquette down pat and know what hosting pitfalls to avoid. All that's left is for you to follow the checklist step-by-step and get to host a delightful, memorable baby shower that the mother-to-be and other guests will remember fondly for years to come.

CPSIA information can be obtained
at www.ICGtesting.com
Printed in the USA
LVOW10s1055260418
574947LV00007BA/108/P

9 781499 271089